AF339304

SYNCHRONIZED SWIMMING

Stephen Corey

1984
Swallow's Tale Press Poetry Award
Co-winner

Additional copies may be obtained by
sending $6.95 plus 50¢ postage, to

Swallow's Tale Press
P.O. Box 4328
Tallahassee, FL 32315-4328

Canada and Mexico, please add 75¢
Payable U.S. funds, please

ISBN 0-930501-01-2
Library of Congress Catalog Number: 85-050561

Printed in the United States of America. Typesetting and printing by
CLS Printing, Tallahassee, FL.

This book is the co-winner of the 1984 Swallow's Tale Press
Poetry Award. The other book is *The Time, The Hour, The
Solitariness of the Place* — a collection of three poetic sequences by
Louis Phillips, which is available from the above address for $7.95,
plus 50¢ postage.

Cover: "Pozzo," by Brandon Kershner.

The editors thank both **Rick Lott** and **Joe Nordgren** for their aid
in judging the 1984 poetry contest.

ACKNOWLEDGEMENTS

Some of the poems in this collection have been published as follows:

The Apalachee Quarterly: "For My First Lover and Her Mother."
The American Poetry Review: "Understanding *King Lear.*"
The Ark: "The Poetry of American Political Tracts."
The Atlanta Gazette: "Listen, My Love."
The Bellingham Review: "Learning to Make Maps," "A Lecture on 'Richard Cory'."
The Beloit Poetry Journal: "Sandlappers," "How Poets Would Have Us Know Them."
California Quarterly: "Divorce."
College English: "Gladys," "Whatever Light."
The Devil's Millhopper: "Ambition and Hate."
The Georgia Review: "Museum of Her Leaving," "Fighting Death," "Bread."
Kansas Quarterly: "The Birth of Christ."
Kudzu: "Spreading My Father's Ashes."
The Louisville Review: "Agnostic," "Inoa Po."
New Collage Magazine: "One Way It Could End," "Understanding the Future," "Chicken in a Florida City."
The New Republic: "Revision."
Pembroke Magazine: "Tu Fu at Pike's Peak."
Poetry: "Freshman Lit & Comp," "Animation," "Preparing to Live Among the Old," "The Uselessness of American Counties."
Southern Humanities Review: "Learning to Live in America," "Music for My Daughters."
Southern Poetry Review: "Deaf and Mute."
Stone Country: "What We Did, What You Will Know," "Third Love Poem," "Two Illusions" (under the title, "Two Ways").
Sun Dog: "Synchronized Swimming," "Pygmalion at Sunrise."
Swallow's Tale: "Georgia O'Keeffe's 'Blue Morning Glories, New Mexico, II'."
Tar River Poetry: "Domestic Life: Nurse and Poet," "Epitaphs," "Religions."
Topo (now *Brushfire*): "The Invention of the Villanelle."
Writer's Digest: "Hearing with My Son."

The second part of this collection, FIGHTING DEATH, was published (in a somewhat different version) in a limited edition chapbook from State Street Press (1983).

Some of the poems from the first and third parts were published in GENTLE IRON LACE, a limited edition chapbook from The Press of the Nightowl (1984).

"Falling in Love at Forty" was published originally in THE LAST MAGICIAN (Water Mark Press, 1981).

The author wishes to thank the following people for their helpful criticism of the manuscript for this book: Barri Armitage, Brandon Kershner, Jr., Stanley Lindberg, Susan Ludvigson, Gene Margo, and Jim Peterson.

The lines on page 35 are quoted from "Skin" by Roland Flint, in *And Morning*, Dryad Press.

The lines on page 9 are quoted from Johan Huizinga's *Homo Ludens*, Rutledge and Kegan, Beacon Press.

CONTENTS

III. WHATEVER LIGHT

SYNCHRONIZED SWIMMING

for my father,

DALE COREY
(1925-1985)

*Even silence must have
its rhythm and shape:
the speech of the newly dead
encompassing the room,
rolling the house
in a stomach-churning swell
across the blackened fields of ice
beyond the black window.*

Synchronized Swimming

After the day's uncertainties, we shape
patterns we are cheered for but cannot see.
Teammates but working alone, we must trust
music and muscle for cadence and touch
to propel our kaleidoscope of limbs,
the flowers and suns of our oiled bodies.
I scull, float, turn, and roll to the dulled beat
reaching me through water. My eye catches
only ceiling, pool-bottom, random breast
or cheek or foot of a girl beside me.
"One body!" coach shouts, again and again.
We must believe ourselves a single form, or fail.

Once, a camera hung like a voyeur
above our opening and closing legs,
but when I saw the film—saw no body
as my own to hold or to fear, no mind
but the sweeping points and circles of flesh—
I cried for happiness in the dark room.

Once, when I left the natatorium
to find myself alone on the steep steps
above the cracked street and scattered lights,
children came to me. They touched me and cheered.
It was as if I could expand for them
there on that grimy stoop, link us all
for some radiant work in the world.

LEARNING TO LIVE IN AMERICA

Sandlappers

*. . . were the poor farmers of the Sand Hills section of
South Carolina. The name comes from the farmers'
fondness for clay-rich sands which they licked to
add starch to their diets.*

Cool evenings we go in families
to lick the earth.
Along the beach in the dim light,
dark clumps of kneelers,
each group carefully apart.
The children balk, but learn.

Once you know the hard-packed places
safe from normal tides,
less grit fills your mouth
than you'd expect. You find a way
to go on. Whenever I bow
I think of my wife's body
in the first years,
how my lips and tongue lifted
all the right tastes from her skin
as if it were hairless and smooth.
I never ask the others their thoughts.
One woman always cries.

Back from the shore,
across the dunes and through the scrub,
corn tassels flip in the wind
while tubers swell slowly beneath.
But in this leached state
what the ground gives is not enough—
we must have the ground itself, or starve.

The Birth of Christ

Beyond the long tables lined with tiny chairs,
the uncurtained stage rises above the lunchroom floor.
Wearing their coats, polite parents sweat through every number.

When two first graders enter alone,
the audience stops its undercurrent mumble.
The girl, head bowed and draped,
watches only the bundle in her arms,
seats herself in the lone chair center-stage.
Joseph follows, shoulders straight, and kneels beside her.

Handel's *Hallelujah* scratches and spreads above us.
Across three hundred years, something reaches
to pull us, shuffling but silent, to our feet.

When the music ends we carry our silence
to the cars by the gym's high wall.
Our dozens of white breaths
puff toward the sky in chorus,
and in the darkness glint the stars
we had not noticed when we came.

Tu Fu at Pike's Peak

An imperishable fame of a thousand years
Is but a paltry, after-life affair.

Who could ever guess
what a man must do
to become a mountain?

I stare from a distance
toward the solitary peak,
chanting the beautiful word
Zebulon, Zebulon.

Small children in bright shirts
scramble on the lowest slopes,
top a ledge, and raise their arms
as if it were the summit.

In Szechwan, a man spent his life
discovering streams in hidden places,
giving every one his name.

Zebulon, Zebulon—
when you journeyed homeward
how much of you returned?
What lay by your wife in the night?

Cars and trailers grind your skin,
oil seeps toward your great heart,
your sweet first name is forgotten.

Did you turn even once from your wife,
from her touch or your children's eyes,
to the mountain you had claimed

like a fool who gathers shiny stones,
then tries to spend them in the marketplace?

In Szechwan the stream-finder died,
an old man beside quick water
that bore his name into the distance.
He did not know which stream that was.
They never found him—never.

The Uselessness of American Counties

Their names are short and ugly,
or long and impossible to spell:
Buck, Dent, Canandaigua.

They only appear on fine state maps—
where they look identical.

Through history, only three did anything
not done better by a city or state.

No young child ever knows he lives in one.
No man, dying, calls one home.

Chicken in a Florida City

There is a chicken outside
the Krispy Kreme doughnut store.
5:00 a.m. tends to be the same
along the suburban avenues
in this medium-sized city,
but this dawn features a chicken.
He paces the concrete surrounding the store.
The workmen keep quiet
as they get their coffee,
but when the young children
begin to arrive at seven o'clock,
they hop and shout, "There's a chicken out there!
Why is there a chicken out there?"
The Egyptian woman behind the counter
leans to see, but can only shrug.
This is not *her* country.
The parents grimace,
press down on their children's shoulders,
and order the usual.
On the way out no one feeds the chicken.
Flour mills still grind in the Midwest,
cane-presses lift sweet winds over the Caribbean.
No customers plan to change their days.
Tomorrow they will come holding dollar bills
and the curious memory of a chicken.

Situation Comedy

Every eleven seconds there is a laugh.
All but necrophilia is allowed:

your oven is covered with frost;
tonight's theater tickets are enroute
to Pittsburgh in my daughter's purse;
you must convince your wife
you've never seen the woman in the closet;
something green and wet is falling
toward the heads of everyone
on-stage for the talent show;
a man lies in his bed all day, hands clenched,
the laugh track rising above his silence.

After the last commercial
a forty second clip resolves it all.
There is no selector knob, no remote control.

Learning to Live in America

One seldom thinks of Delaware,
yet surely as the Tetons rise
in any painting, starving dogs
like unicorns roam the streets
of Wilmington, and cabbies joust
on freeways no smaller than our own.
None of us knows anyone
who has walked in North Dakota,
but our glove compartments overflow
with maps we've collected, lined for Bismarck.
We must be ready for Missouri—
the European countries it will hold
in silhouette, the soggy issue of *Time*
in a St. Joseph alleyway,
the girl by the river whose breast glistens
from the touch of her lover's tongue.

The Poetry of American Political Tracts

- for Emily Dickinson and Walt Whitman

The Japanese used to compose the weightiest part of a State document in poetic form.

- Johan Huizinga -

The Articles of Confederation
to be recast in heroic couplets,
the Declaration of Independence
as a Shakespearian sonnet sequence,
the Constitution in loose-lined blank verse
(*We the people of the United States*)
with amendments in westernized haiku.

All subsequent laws and judicial decisions
In freer rhythms--form following function--
until the images of America
crystallize on the bodies of the people
as eagle feathers. Then,
swimming plashless on banks of noon
we look to where our boot-soles left the earth
and hear the prints of brown return to green.

Georgia O'Keeffe's "Blue Morning Glories, New Mexico, II"

Two blossoms, four times natural size.
The one behind opens to the sky, petals
floating like fronds of underwater plants.
Yet for all its large beauty, pale
yellow and white rising into soft, deep blue,
it remains distant, chooses the sun.
The front one blares toward us with its glow—
a gramophone speaker heard through gauze.
In radiant yellow some new language
pours up from the hidden calyx.
No flower has ever been painted before.
If we can wait, we might see Dante emerge
from this shining, his climb to the sky complete.

FIGHTING DEATH

Steam

Never takes the straight path,
but sways and coils in a white dance
to the end of its world.
Waters the garden of your hand
high above the coffee.
Pretends to be smoke
but doesn't suffocate,
pretends to be winter breath
as it burns your cheek.
Like flames in the fireplace
rises from your cup
to mesmerize, and warm your hands.
Like a love dissolved, never returns
though you stare a hole through the sky.

Listen, My Love

Listen to Edward.
Edward says I write beautiful poems about love.
He is jealous.
He keeps plotting love poems,
but they keep drifting away
to death, politics, trees.
Edward fears his women leave him,
or never come to him,
because he cannot tell their stories.
He cannot hold them in his poems—
their hands slide off
into political-spectrum symbols,
their bodies become bored as bodies
and turn into rural landscapes.
When I say what my hands feel on you
that they feel nowhere else,
Edward rages with respect.
Every time his hand enters one of his poems,
the flesh drops away.
I comfort him. What he does is good, necessary.
We write of what we fear
or do not understand.

For My First Lover and Her Mother

The traffic light's colors change in the air
above my car stalled by the hospital.
How we are growing undoes what we are—

up in that room with flowers and cancer,
the wall of her mother's room reflects all
the traffic light's colors. Change in the air

is fog beginning, is her daughter's hair
spreading across seven years to recall
how we are. Growing undoes what we are—

you raise your husband's lust someplace out there,
here your mother's cells harvest a ripe hell.
The traffic light's colors change. In the air

the moon shines like your belly's taut skin where
his unborn child presses against my skull—
how we are growing undoes what we are.

You've lain in her stomach and in this car—
all things come down to the strength of a cell.
The traffic light's colors change in the air.
How we are growing undoes what we are.

The Invention of the Villanelle

A tall man lost everything,
started talking to himself.
Found a phrase that comforted,
spoke it now and then for grief.
The words turned against him, pained him.
He found a phrase to fight them with.
Days on end he walked the streets
chanting and taken for mad.
Low-lying clouds pressed down gray,
compacted his grief and speech—
two phrases, four times each,
to save his life. His chanting
taken as music, madness as form.

THREE POEMS

I. Falling in Love at Forty

One needs it more now.
Adolescence has so much else
to keep itself feeling young.

Yukio Mishima,
approaching middle age,
wrote in his diary
"Today I have learned to move
a new abdominal muscle."

Perhaps I must ask
no more nor less than this:
that the backs of my hands
become suddenly strange,
that I may study them
as my palms enclose your face,
that the veins of what was always mine
somehow come back to me again.

II. What We Did, What You Will Know

We invented a language
you will never speak,
but you will hear its diction
in all I can write.
Any scholar of my work
will know, for every word,
one less thing than you.
You will know a candle means
a tall gray bookcase,
any small wound is a rug,
and orange shirts are ropes
that can pull us to places
different from those we have known.

III. Third Love Poem

Having resolved to wait for things of worth
before daring to speak, having said two ways
the single night we had those months ago,
I have held my silence as I would a broom
in a dark and spotless room. But tonight
my mind is what my skin was
in that place of rugs and candles,
and once again I am the poet
of emptiness held off, of four hands
astonished by the tricks they could play.

Pygmalion at Sunrise

The morning after.
Sitting pale on his bed's edge,
back turned on the sleeping,
breathing girl.

Sitting this way since before dawn.
Dares not look at her—
fears some ruse of the gods.

Yesterday the statue in his workshop,
last evening came living Galatea.
Why not, this morning, in a world of such gods,
the death-face of Medusa?

Two Illusions

I. A Change

Suppose you were not used to wind
passing through the bedroom. Suppose,
for one moment when you woke that day,
you thought it was her, rushing to your life.

II. No Change

You thought it was breeze through the window,
waking you in some new way. But then
it was her hair grazing your face, no
change, the same hair, again and again.

Nothing but Love Poems Now

You would know why this happens—
why I turn my back to drunks,
refuse to sing with my children,
narrow the world brutally
every time I speak.

For years I believed
in choice, in molding a life
where truth, kindness, and guilt, ignored,
would cut like nails in my shoe.

Now I believe in the rough
swelling disc of your nipple
soft against my obedient tongue,

the words you form to tell me
my life as it's never been,

your eyes' black clamps on my pen.

Deaf and Mute

Safe beyond the edge of the country
we walk the streets and beaches of this island,
off-season guests holding hands fiercely,
inviting the sparse crowd to know that we are lovers.

An old and very local museum
falls victim to our constant laughter
as we tour its chaotic displays:
Beneath the photo of a 1920's bowling team,
a glass case with one cow's skull,
one rusted shovel, and one tin bucket.
Handwritten cards beside them read,
respectively, "Old," "Very Old," and "Ancient."
Down the hall, a foot-high copy of the *Pietá*
sits atop a case of military medals;
above the Lord, a photograph of the smiling,
monocled comedian, Charles Coburn.

The old deaf curator missed our giggles.
Your breathing and moaning do not pass
beyond this room. On the nightstand
your watchstrap arcs the left lens of my glasses,
both dwarfed by the pink telephone.

And now you sleep curled on your side,
hands tucked beneath your cheek, lips parted.
And I sit watching those lips: everything
they are not saying, all the sense
they cannot make until they touch my skin.
Before today, have we ever heard or said
a single word we could not live without?

Religions

Like the shock of waking
into the flash of sun
on a day we've been promised rain.

Like glancing at your watch,
then staring as you find the time
to be earlier than you'd thought—
your life expanded by an hour.

Like walking back toward the table
from the men's room off in the hall,
returning to see the restaurant
siphoned of light by her face—
the customers watching her,
stunned by the one beauty
I've never been able to speak.

To My Queen as We Age

My brothers called me bumbler, simpleton, child.

When the king called for treasure
they went thrashing through the world,
trampled what they might have won.
I stood still until the ground split
before me, entered to piles of gold,
earned your hand.

When the king called for peace
my brothers charged from the kingdom,
only to return pursued.
I watered dry earth, fed dying birds,
pulled a struggling lion from the slough:
briars and thistles slowed the enemy,
nets dropped from the sky held him,
fangs killed him.

My brothers and your father gone,
you call for the final prize:
a heart against time and loneliness.
As always, there is nowhere to search
beyond my reach or out of sight.
Your face, once touched by my hand,
will return when this withered king's cry
goes out for any softness.
Look at me now,
and as all the world's fools
stumble off to nothing,
the rock of my eyes
will split for you, forever.

FIGHTING DEATH

I. Museum of Her Leaving

He was collecting things of air—
life preservers, bubbles of soap, balloons—
so their form, emptiness enclosed,
could remind him of her going.

What first demanded search
soon came calling with offerings of air:
His room. His house. Each lawn from there
three hundred miles down the coast.
The world. His lungs. Asking to be filled
with their precious nothing, drained
by cries across the aging table
splintered by scrapings of a thousand cups and plates
in her thousand hands.

II. Understanding the Future

The piano begins to play,
discordant before the dawn.
You leave your silent book
to enter the living room
where the cat is in flight
to the floor. You know
she has walked the keys,
yet can prove nothing.
You try to close the piano
but strike the board,
raising the same random sound
that jarred your empty night.
Beyond the fading resound of the room
your family sleeps down the long hall,
and you have lost
the one woman
who could carry you through to the end.

III. Fighting Death

> *And if I die, who will write*
> *My poems to you,*
> *Who will utter the sound*
> *Of my still-unspoken words?*
>
> - Anna Akhmatova -

1

Once, bullets clicked the leaves above us,
random shots from an unseen hunter.
Our eyes locked as we dressed lying flat.
As we hunched away—I sent you first,
a rare chivalry in my life—
the sounds were so tiny, so clean,
I knew we would be safe.

2

We hated the ocean so always went,
its boring slosh and frightening green
turning us toward ourselves. We walked the beach
as the blind stride the rooms of their own homes,
knowing that nothing will stand in the way.

3

Two others we would call children
walk linked along the street,
her hand curved in his hip pocket,
his elbow resting on her shoulder.
Her long black hair scatters in the wind,

slapping softly against them both.
If I call to them, they will hurry off.

4

I sit with words like a kitten
on a floor full of playthings,
leaping from one to another
sparked more by muscle than thought.
Each reach for your love is one
last pull on the slot machine.
Sometime in second grade I learned
I could count till the day I died
but never dent the system.
To speak to you forever,
I would even believe in God.

Animation

What to do now with the magical turtles?
The ones who slipped from their shells
to race down the road on skinny legs
toward the unsuspecting hare,
then eased back in when the race was won.
What to do with exploding dogs and cats?
Their eyeballs and limbs flying apart
in the face of the cartoon's ghost,
till snapping back like rubber bands.

I keep walking away from the form
I gained by your presence and skin,
as if a building could hop
from its own foundation
and hike to Wyoming or Maine.
Every few steps I accordion down
to the ground, recalling as I wilt
that I do, indeed, have a basis
in the world, a namesake in history:
I am the fool unzipped in his sleep
by the wily one, my skeleton
slipped out whole and hung
in a place I can see but cannot reach.

One Way It Could End

Your body has become the ideal
grim spokesman for dying:
your flaccid chest of dry hairs,
your dull bone mask a thing
women stare past or turn from quietly.
Then, in the last moments,
she is there again as you knew her
forty-one years before: her hair
a long shining fall
from the arm of that couch to the floor,
as if black were sun,
as if nothing ends.
You try to see her in the yellow
pall of your own palm,
but her absence holds her tight
in a past your sadness cannot crack.
And so you surrender,
set your lips to the breasts and dreams
she was and is—is—
and you die.

Divorce

When you die in a northern town
our two graying daughters call me home.
Driving in, I find the strange
countryside and town the same
as places where we met: endless
hills of maple, pine, corn and cattle,
red-brick streets, high wood-frame houses.
I arrive with my second wife,
my thirty years with her
twice what I had with you.
Only my daughters know me—
our friends different, parents dead,
other relations afraid to come.
Nothing I've known prepared me
for this moment at your grave.
Your second husband four years dead,
I feel, for the first time,
I must be yours again.
Nevermind our thirties,
when youth unravelled
to its opposites—selfishness and fear.
Once, you talked and kissed
only that I might remember, and I do.
By the stone you share with him
my arms encircle our daughters.
Their heads press my chest
in the vice I have avoided
for so long: difficult love.
The rows of stones radiate from yours.
The sun shone for your burial.
The maples here look healthy,
yet the tips of many branches
hang snapped, as if a storm
had passed through yesterday.

As ever, I don't know how to leave—
which last words to blurt across this mound,

which woman to clutch as I turn,
which wrong choice to make once more.

33

Domestic Life: Nurse and Poet

- for Mary -

We talk tonight as if tomorrow will be the same,
as if we'll rise at six to get the children off,
then work the day—I with words and students,
you with the sick, the dying, and their desperate families—
until we come home at five to unleash the dog
and feed the children. We expect we'll read to them,
shush them resisting off to bed, sit here on the couch
to talk once more. We are thirty-three, but the world
mistakes you always for six or seven less.
Tonight you smile—nobody died today.
Beneath your eyes only inches away,
I catch for the first time tiny marks,
hairbreadth engravings of a stylus on copper.
On another they would be lines,
but on you, tonight, while we consider tomorrow
and who can hurry home to meet the plumber,
they are the tightening muscles in my gut,
the faults in the deepest beds of rock.

Belief

- for Roland Flint -

> *somehow*
> *in between the wood and wine*
> *there will be no separation,*
> *wood from dark from wine.*

Because my home is long I read your poem
that night as I walked from bedroom to hallway
to foyer. The light in the corridor
faded toward the front of the house.
Your words on the page grew dim,
so when I reached the black doorway
the last word on the page
was the last I could have read—
as if this were the perfect poem,
its wood and wine in step with my life,
the seamless end shivering my skin
because when the doctor said it was a daughter
I was kneeling by my wife's face,
and for a moment, while I had to wait
for his hands to lift from between her legs,
I was father and not-father, with nothing
but belief to tip me either way,
to show me my new life and my old at once,
with nothing but belief joining
the rooms of every home we walk.

Counseled by His Readers to Abandon Love Lyrics and Take Up the Real Work of the World in His Writing, He Responds

Say it: a dream saves nothing, walks nowhere—
carries no wood to the thick walls of peace,
to the delicate fires of justice.

Say it: the heart is the greatest trickster,
hawking a lilting form of the world
while small stomachs ache and the dust descends.

Tell me: truth's a bare patch on a distant hill,
a lost spot hidden from my engines of words
gliding the roads on their honey-slick wheels.

Chide me with visions converted to bone:
Laura, Dark Lady, young Fanny, Maud Gonne.
Quote me the sum of lovers reborn through metaphor.

But listen: if the heart were helium
it would lift me clear of your notions—
sail me, shrinking but shining, toward the evening clouds.

WHATEVER LIGHT

Ambition and Hate

-for several friends-

You ain't nothing without the right ambition

*****

You ain't nothing without the right hate

(local graffiti)

I. For R.P.D.

Some foreign city glints below—
a fourteen-story drop to the snow
covering the streets and the Boston Commons.
This is April, but no spring blossoms
in memory of salty tea, of Revere,
of a complex dream that started here
and sprawled across the San Andreas Fault.

We have come to this cold history book
for a *convention* of writers, struck
hardly at all by such an irony.
Most of us travel in flocks to parties,
restaurants, lectures and museums,
pleased by the changes of scene that hum
in all our senses. But you—you hate Boston.

"Everything bad that ever happened
happened here before I was eight."
On Thursday you swear this visit,

39

your first in twenty years, is the last
for twenty more. By Saturday you've guessed
an old hotel where your father hid away
before he died. You might come back to stay.

The uncaught man who murdered your father,
the cancerous lung of your mother
six months later—these were the engines of hate
in a small boy's heart, pistons so great
you could only move on by forgetting
they were always there. But now, their sting
rises through you at fifty-four in this frozen
Boston spring, and what you hate must be chosen,
confronted as the one way forward and back.

II. For J.G.

> *He has gone where fierce indignation*
> *can lacerate his heart no more*

On our strong and optimistic days
we could believe that such an epitaph
would crown and justify a life,
atone for any sadness that could rise
from our anger at a world whose chaos
not even Swift, so bilious, could devise.

In the lobby of this grand hotel
you find hydrangeas dying in a windowbox.
Carelessness at the core of opulence
is a fragile, deadly form you know too well:
the choking of the sea, the burning acid of the air,
the radiant refuse in the bomb of the earth.
As you picket and march and write, your grim faith
is the lioness blocking the mouth to the lair,
standing up to a dozen guns or lances
to gain the last few moments for her young.

You lament hydrangeas in a lonely tongue
whose lexicon is tenderness laced
with anger, the whole speech dropped on a starched cashier
who mouths the world's dreary song—
fault gone elsewhere, well-meaning and empty-faced.
I cannot conceive, much less begin, a comfort to your rage.

III. For D.H.

Keats by his brother's deathbed, breathing
day after day the consumptive air
that would kill him if he left or stayed—
the lush words of a lifetime traded
for the silence of pain, for hair
curled and wet on Tom's pale forehead. Sing
we mustn't, through fear of disturbing
Tom's slow drift into babble—yet sing
we must, for John and his selfless care:
ready to best Milton and Shakespeare,
knowing his greatness was there, a fine thread
he must cut himself like a stray hair
let fall from a window on the evening air.
And no one to touch, or pursue, or hate, but the dead.

The Vital and the Trivial of Our Days

The special trick grip I learned as a child—
slotting my thumbnail and forefinger nail
to the slick red grooves of the toothpaste cap,
then flicking it off in that special way
I've never seen equalled or neared.

Driving my daughters to school, then wishing
them well for the day by biting my tongue—
thinking my silence is the only way
to clear them for what they must find.

The lover I haven't touched in seven years,
the one I wouldn't dare to come across
for fear of all the mirrors she would be—
she rises in me once again, useless
as charred pine, insistent as hunger's buzz.

Certain museums have special closed boxes
(for children's amusement, we're generally told),
with samples of rock that take flashes of light
we set off with buttons while peering through holes.
A rock goes red, goes blue, goes dark,
according to the light we use.

Art Elective

Reflex of memory thrusts
the strong-voweled name *Rouault*
out through my lips as I walk
the hall of my daughter's school
and sight his poster on the wall—
the blocky reds and browns
surrounded by swaths of black,
the squat figures angry
yet somehow sanctified.
I am reminded of style,
how it is rarely taught
but never mistaken once learned,
how I came to it in high school
through luck of scheduling, through Art
Appreciation class—that lone elective
slotted among the requirements.

Old Miss Proctor, green smock
spattered to stringy rainbows,
walked the room like a Pollock miniature.
Her hunched back and wizened face,
the long tables in place of desks,
the full wall of windows—
at first, the class seemed a kindergarten
break, a ball-and-wire cartoon,
Miró amid the testing and the bells.

But Amy was there beside me,
our knees touching beneath the table
we shared in the back-right row.
Our loving scholastic war,

three years old, had never been
so serious and gently fierce
as in those months we learned to sense
the bronze and glow of Rembrandt, to see
the soft-toned lumps of apples and hills—
almost interchangeable, almost alive—
in the many-angled lightings of Cezanne.

The rest of the school was so carefully lit
to protect itself and all of us
from the little darks we were, or might become;
but in Art Appreciation
the dark became the learning space,
holding back the regular light
so the slides could shine and brood
on the luminescent screen above us.
My fingertips were on Amy's thigh,
coming up under her skirt to the edge
where stocking met skin, stunning
border—her hand on me showing
what my hand was doing for her.

Miss Proctor at the bright screen's edge,
pointer and fingers reaching out
to the special blush of blue
that meant Vermeer, "That will mean Vermeer,"
she said, "until the end of the world."
Here, removed from corridors
lined by dull green lockers,
Van Gogh's fiery hills and pinwheels
swirled above the Thirteen Colonies,
the rubbery frogs, the cosines, and the verbs—
and this, we came to know, is style:
the heart of a hand and eye,
knowable though unpredictable,
the shapes and shades we acquire
both with and against our wills.

As if need were impediment to learning,
our careful parents lectured us in love—
how it was still a choice for the young,

something not yet hardened by necessity.
But from Blake's acid-etched flames and flowers
arose the palpable words we sought:
You never know what is enough
unless you know what is more than enough.

While others dawdled and stalled
as if nothing here were tangible,
Amy and I sought perfect scores.
Hour by hour after school
we studied the paintings and sculpture again,
studied the curious notes we'd taken
with our free hands in the dark:
a dozen grids by Mondrian,
his primary colors ruled like cloth
exposed by a microscope;
Gauguin's brown and solid bodies,
ominous and awkward paradise.
And Miss Proctor there at our shoulders,
pressing us even with diction:
"Each piece and detail," she said,
"becomes a synecdoche of style."

For just one week she made us
artists, workers in the crafts we observed.
Chalk on heavy paper was my choice,
symbolic abstraction my excuse
for a hand not linked with eye:
a thick, red cross hung high
against blackened air, purple hills
set far below; a jagged graph-line, green,
descending through the cross, moving
left to right into the hills.
The title: "History of Man."
Our final day I abandoned the work,
slashed it with spirals of chalk.
Miss Proctor took it up, championed
its power—swirls and all—to the class.
Amy's thigh gave pressure to mine.
I sat silent, took credit, knowing

Miss Proctor did not believe in accident.
(Her first day's words: *I am an artist.*
My name is Florence.)

I know a man of superb intelligence
who cannot bring himself to eat
a strawberry, although he loves the taste.
As a child he was stricken
by the clear resemblance of strawberries
to his uncle's pocked and bulbous nose;
four decades have not lessened his fear,
his sense of immoral desire . . . .

I watch this poster of Rouault
but see my friend's perverse distress.
I would wish that nose away, would change it
to the breast of my friend's finest lover,
would give him the piling up, the layering,
concocted of dream upon resonant dream—
the writhings of fact made real.

Stephen Corey

Synchronized Swimming

Publication: April 20, 1985
Price: 6.95 postpaid
60 pages, paperback
ISBN 0-930501-01-2

Louis Phillips

The Time, The Hour,
The Solitariness of the Place
three sequences

Publication: Sept. 30, 1985
Price: 7.95 postpaid
75 pages, paperback
ISBN 0-930501-02-0

Swallow's Tale Press Poetry Winners

1985 Rules:
- Prize of $500 plus book publication
- At least 48 pages, manuscript.
- Deadline is May 29, 1985
- Include S.A.S.E.
- Manuscript may be entered in other contests.
- 6.00 entry fee required.
- All entrants will receive a copy of the winning book.
- No entry forms necessary. See reverse side for address.

The Copper Monkey Is One

The Copper Monkey, darkened
restaurant we loved, partly,
because we never knew
the meaning of its name.

That day, your face
misted by the dimness
though only a foot away
across the fragile wooden table.
The black of your hair
shaming the room's thin darkness,
falling past your face
and down across your breasts—
the taste and softness I had dreamed
through fifteen years of others,
but never imagined, really,

until you turned them toward me
two years before The Copper Monkey,
turned toward me
as you dropped your dress—
it hung for that instant
on your nipples, then fell—
as you dropped your dress
and raised your eyes
in that other quiet room.

But in The Copper Monkey
your hair was across your breasts
and below the table's edge,

with nothing to keep me
from believing that soft, black anchor
might descend into the earth forever.
Needing to keep back something
I offered up a charm to hold you:
"I am thinking something great
and frightening. Five years from now,
wherever we are, ask what I thought
that day in The Copper Monkey."
As if what I would not say
could have drawn you toward me.

Two months later we lay
in a field of purple phlox,
you on your stomach beneath me,
pressing my chest and groin
as if I were the one beneath,
or the earth upon us both.
Your breathing, slow and wordless,
recalled me to The Copper Monkey,
and in that moment there was nothing
I could have in the world
without giving it over to you:
"That day in The Copper Monkey
your face was so perfect
the thought of what five years would do
was more losing than I could stand.
The only chance was staring more
at your beautiful face that would change."

And now, five times five years later,
I see The Copper Monkey is one
remembrance among the many
we must build—so many
that even the slowest death
cannot last longer
than our calling up of these pictures and tales.

Hearing with My Son

*Our studies show that the autistic child apparently
has a random relationship with sounds, linking
them with whatever object holds his attention at
the moment.*

Crouched by his chair, my son hears
my complaint from the wine glass,
my praise from his own shoe.
When I read him books, I speak
through their pictures, or the wall.

Despite my love, I say less and less—
even if he heard me in the trees
or the sunset, he would not listen.

Perhaps, somewhere on the soft and hot
savannahs of Kenya, a newborn gazelle
speaks with the voice of my son.

He throws his cup across the room.
His hand explodes with the crash.

FOR MY DAUGHTERS

Inoa Po

One name whispered by the gods
past the hill of the rounded belly:
the given, perfect sound for the child
to carry as comfort and yearning,
the homing pigeon's single place
in the chaos of air and earth.

Come sit on my lap, Miranda.
Miranda, where have you been?
What are you doing, Miranda?
Miranda . . . Miranda.
Be home before dark, Miranda.

If the name we give is wrong
the curses will descend,
and the child cannot answer
whenever the gods may call.
So many other ways to fail,
no excuse to let down on this—
give ear to the hillside, ear to the wind,
to the name of the name for now.

Learning to Make Maps

- for Miranda at 7 -

Line for the driveway,
box for the church,
bigger box the parking lot,
squiggles the carport pick-up zone:

your freehand map to lead me
later through the dark
to a place not mine but yours,
shared with a neighbor's child,
regimen of Wednesday nights.

If you've drawn others
I cannot remember when.
This is your mind moving
through the world at last,
going to its places,
bringing its places home.

I remember, from the back seat,
watching my father navigate
the red-brick city streets
and empty country roads
as if he'd never lose the way. . . .

Go on now, in the neighbor's car,
to whatever rites present themselves
to your small and lovely face.
I will be there when you finish.
I promise this map will do.

Music for My Daughters

Beyond all our bounds of monotony
the child lies down each night
to the same record on the tiny machine,
her drowsing and dreams evolving
week after week from identical songs.
She neither thinks of how she chose this theme,
nor perceives she will sometime choose another,
but knows she cannot sleep with silence.
When the time comes suddenly for change
she leaves the old music without regret,
with scarcely a thought of the shift—
since the heart of her comfort, the voice
lifted far past daily speech, remains.

Understanding *King Lear*

When you stir
the blueberry yogurt—

spoon down through
the white cultured yogurt
to the syrup and fruit
underneath,

dark bluepurple rising
first in bursts of color,
then swirling as you stir
into designs of thin-lined
purple and white,

distinction fading
to a deep magenta cream
lumped with blue,
magenta-covered berries—

imagine
Shakespeare's life,
the daily incidents,
the human brilliance.

Freshman Lit & Comp

-for Janet Burroway-

Wednesday evenings rooted to his place
—back row, nearest the door—
he had that plodding obstinance
of dullness laced with purpose.
Past twenty-five, pimpled and flabby,
bursting out of himself
at every tuck and button.
Arriving and leaving alone.

Never an answer, never a question,
hauling himself toward me every week
from the wood-lathe of his job
in a low grade furniture shop,
ready for commas, Milton, paragraphs, Donne.
Every other week, another essay
into listlessness and error,
as if the writing meant no more
than the grease he carried on his cuffs.

The Iliad provided the finish.
Six years later, I still can paint
the slants and tones of sunlight
mapped across my desk, or sing
the fossils deep below me
in those moments when I read
his final thesis of our course:

>That the truest choice by Homer
>was the crippling of Hephaestus,
>for only the damaged could understand
>the shield scrolled with gentle iron lace,
>the aura that holds around the perfect forging.

A Lecture on "Richard Cory"

The brilliance of complete things
we often find resides, actually,
in a single piece of the whole.
As in "Richard Cory," where the horrible
power is in the simple word *put*.

    And Richard Cory, one calm summer night,
    Went home and put a bullet through his head.

Not *blasted*, not *fired*, not even *drove*.
We can envision a man
holding a bullet between fingers and thumb,
and pushing it into his brain.
The splitting of the skull, the gush of blood,
the slow grinding through bone
until the slug pops easily
into the soft cortex.
This is a man *putting* a bullet—
a man getting through another moment
of his life, one which is coincidentally,
as it turns out, the last he will ever know.

Gladys

Something in her sharp face made me nervous.
I was seventeen—my first time-card work—
and each morning when I punched in, Gladys
was there on her stool near the loading dock.
She was a sander, handling tiny parts
die-cast at the rear of the plant: levers
for voting machines, hasps of twenty sorts.
Working piece-rate, her fingers were fliers
near my gimp thumbs on the huge press machine.
I trimmed waste like an axe-man dropping heads,
she soothed and buffed steel with a touch so fine
you'd wish her always in your midnight bed.
But her face—the first I'd seen with youth so thin
I stared each morning to see if it was gone.

Preparing to Live Among the Old

Go where there is music,
whether to parks and streets
with sun on flashing brass,
or darkened bars in jukebox glow.
This is your gentle beginning:
in the presence of song nearly all forgive
the wheezing voice and sagging heart.

Almost without your noticing,
allow no hand, year upon year,
to stroke or touch your skin.

Spend your days in a single room.
Imagine your walls as mirrors
reflecting mirrors behind you.
Wherever you look you will see,
past eyes and rounded shoulders,
your curving back, faceless—
a stranger you will not meet again.

Bread

-for Susan-

There will be bread no matter what,
so you choose to mourn with flour
powdering your hairline,
with your hands shredded by strings of dough.
You can dream the desert of Moses,
the beehive ovens of Africa,
the softest *croissants* of erotic days—
anything but this chilling house,
the death of your closest friend.
You mourn through the beat of your hands' kneading,
for the unbroken history of bread
is neither accident nor wonder,
but the survival of simplicity:
bread was our purest creation,
flour transformed by water and fire.

Someone watching from across the yard
or high above the reddening autumn trees
could not know what special grain you breed—
the sour tang of rye, the sweet heaviness of white—
but would know each grows from grief,
that single soil we always walk.

As the smooth loaves warm and swell
under the dampened cloth, and the oven's heat
drifts to adjoining rooms, you give yourself
a moment to believe in miracles.
But your aching hands recall you

to the work this day has been,
while the dried and cracking film of dough
stiffens your fingers until they seem,
themselves, the residue of failure.
In the burning water from the faucet
you scrub your skin and scrape your nails
as if somehow they could come to match
the rising gold of the oven's loaf.

But the full beauty of bread
resides in its consumption,
and you know the threat of weeks to come:
you will raise a hand to point directions,
or you will circle your lover's neck
until your hand comes close to your face:
and there, buried beneath the nail
like a shard of your own bones,
the last dried speck of dough—
the savior that cracks your heart.

Spreading My Father's Ashes

We touch again—
my hand dips and clutches,
fist full
yet fingers nearly down flat
against the palm.
Hand raised, fingers sprung.

You phony bastard,
why didn't you tell them
about this place—
tell them how you loved it?
Big-shit Swede,
off the boat and into the money:
"Know more about their money than they do,
they'll have to share it with you."
Philosopher, disguised as phony bastard
Certified Public Accountant.

Dropping becomes throwing
as the path circles back to the cabin,
the circuit of the land
more finished than the task.
I aim for things, but miss.
A windshift fires one throwing
straight back in my face.

Crazy son-of-a-bitch,
head of the firm,
long workdays torn by debit and credit,
raging existentialism once each year
at your office Christmas party
on a quart of Scotch,

preaching to dazed CPAs
the death of God, the joke of Christ—

then driving drunk to this place,
sleeping it all off,
waking to a snowy day of great peace.

Last shaking and whacking,
the upside-down urn;
hands rinsed by icy pump-water,
dried with broad rubbings across old jeans.
My hands are clean.

I watch the damp on my thighs,
the water-darkened cloth
streaked white by faint remnants of ash.

Agnostic

A god would have given some task to the dead.
One wouldn't ask for much,
just some break from the stillness and dark.
To have them forever dancing on distant hillsides
would be a comfort, but too much to expect.
Yet they could have been allowed
some quiet action—gardening in small fenced yards,
or sitting at our windows, looking out
at the movement in streets and fields.

Revision

He riffles manuscripts
from years so far behind
he recalls them only,
now and then, as a lifting
of the eye, a distant
dry spark across the neck
where once his skin had learned
to expect such burning gifts.

Pausing to read one sheet
he discovers verses
immeasurably bad,
but then, just halfway down,
discerns one line of thought
still equal to his need—
except for one wrong word,
an *a* that should be *the*.

He pencils in the change,
then drops a hundred sheets
back down upon this one
and packs them all away.
Across the yard and fields,
the orange sun cracks upward
as if it sensed the broad expanse
whose darkness it would fill.

Water-Shadow

We know not why or what, yet weave, forever weave.

- Walt Whitman -

On a sunny day it would be shadow,
this needle-fine web of moisture
near the pavement's edge
beneath the evergreens.
But dew and later clouds
made the pines protect the road today
not from glare but from drying,
leaving this lace of water
as a fossil of the night.

Though asphalt and earth ask nothing,
I could bare my chest and lay it
against this odd morning map.
The deep weave of my veins
would match the earth as if mirrored—
a moment of dreams and regrets,
the thoughts of a Siamese twin
as the surgeon's knife comes down.

Epitaphs

> —in memory of John Hamilton Reynolds (1794-1852),
> who chose to be identified on his tombstone
> only as *The Friend of Keats*—

We all have this final chance to speak:
Here, under the wide oaks preserved
as if shade and coolness were honor
for the dead. Or here, in this flat space
burning beneath the sun, open
to that sun as only broad water
should be open. Or here, crowded
upon a tilted, corroding stone
in sight of the country church.

Books and letters can serve, shelved
apart from acid and ice and rain,
but only our last stone words can rest
within sounding distance of our bones.
We need science but no religion to know
how the timbre and pitch of any voice,
reciting our words with face bent downward,
will pass waves through the ground—
will resonate against us
in the pattern of our chosen sounds.
Yet we opt for the relative silence
put forth by a name and two dates,
or we settle for standardized blessings:

God-fearing Man

*

Dear, Loving Mother

*

Resting This Hour with God

John Hamilton Reynolds, I say
there are better voices than these—
better for the human, for any divines.

Something from our own repeated speech:

> *18 seasons*
> *with the pharmacy softball team,*
> *13 and 12 in our only winning year.*
> *
> *Janice, where in the hell*
> *are my goddamned shoes?*

Something from what we had meant to say:

> *Whenever you were not looking,*
> *for all those years,*
> *I studied the ways of light*
> *against your hair.*

Or something we would never speak
in any other place or way:

> *For all I knew and tried,*
> *I never learned to distinguish*
> *silence from truth,*
> *speech from the urge to speak.*

Yet for you, Reynolds, The Friend of Keats,
not even these would have been enough.
Walk away to the world,
you seem to have said.
Set another, always, before you.

The sun and the mirror serve,
but must not be stared at.

How Poets Would Have Us Know Them

As we read calligraphy,
where pressure, angle, and nib
free beauty from sense.

As we shiver
to the voice of a certain singer,
always wanting more,
nevermind the words.

As we rise
to a lover's hand as it nears,
though we do not know
what the stroke this time will be—
though the lover may be gone,
the hand in our dreams alone.

Whatever Light

You dreamed the sound of your own name
was imbued with resonance,
could be offered to the world
just as you could stand at the curb
on a side street in Wichita
saying quietly, every few seconds,
"Shakespeare …Shakespeare… Shakespeare."
And you could leave knowing
you had touched some feeling
in nearly all who passed your slow chant:
The fat woman in the green dress
whose only boyfriend years before had tried
in earnest to recite the balcony scene.
The man who once walked howling from his broken home,
his dying daughter in his arms.

But you awoke to a name of no music or charm,
one that would roll from the bed
to stand alone waiting for first light
through the valanced brown curtains.
You knew that the glowing or dullness
in that day's particular light
would alter the tone of your voice.
You knew, whatever the light,
you would enter it that day
to speak to whatever ears
might still hear the music
you knew must exist.

Born in Buffalo and raised in Jamestown, New York, **Stephen Corey** earned his B.A. (1971) and M.A. (1974) in English at the State University of New York at Binghamton (Harpur College). From 1972-1975 he worked as a reporter for the Jamestown *Post-Journal*, and in 1975 he and his family moved to Gainesville, Florida, where he completed his Ph.D. in English (1979).

His first published poem appeared in 1976 in *A Local Muse*, an anthology of Gainesville poetry edited by visiting poets Stephen Spender and Robert Dana. The following year, Corey and Edward Wilson founded *The Devil's Millhopper*. Corey co-edited that poetry journal with Wilson (1977-1978) and with Lola Haskins (1978-1981) before becoming editor (1981-1983). He left *The Devil's Millhopper* to become Assistant Editor of *The Georgia Review*, at the University of Georgia, where he is today.

The Last Magician, his first book of poems, was selected by Charles Fishman to be published as the 1981 winner of the Water Mark Press Poets Award. Two chapbooks followed: *Fighting Death* (State Street Press, 1983) and *Gentle Iron Lace* (Press of the Nightowl, 1984). From 1976-1985, Corey's poems have appeared in such magazines as *The American Poetry Review*, *Beloit Poetry Journal*, *The Georgia Review*, *The New Republic*, and *Poetry*.

Mr. Corey has published criticism and reviews in *Virginia Quarterly Review*, *The Georgia Review*, *Poet and Critic*, *South Atlantic Journal*, *Alaska Quarterly Review*, and elsewhere. He lives in Athens, Georgia with his wife, Mary Elizabeth, and his two daughters, Heather and Miranda.

This collection is the co-winner of the 1984 Swallow's Tale Press Poetry Award. It and Louis Phillips' collection were selected for publication from well over two hundred entries.

Brandon Kershner's photograph "Pozzo" is incorporated into the cover for this book. Mr. Kershner teaches English at the University of Florida and has been semi-professionally involved in photography for the last five years. His own poetry has appeared in many magazines including *American Poetry Review* and *Poetry*, and he has published, with Todd Walker, a book called *Dialogues*, a collection of poetry and photography.